AF428703

Death of the Dollar

A Watchman's Warning

Economic Shaking and the Convergence of Control

By

Laura Lindsey

ISBN:
978-8-9954070-0-3 — Paperback
978-8-9954070-1-0 — Hardback
978-8-9954070-2-7 — Ebook (EPUB)

Dedication

To the remnant.

To the watchmen on the wall.

To the believers who sense the shaking but refuse to fear it.

To those who love Jesus more than comfort, security, or status.

To my family, my greatest earthly blessing, who remind me daily that courage and faith begin at home.

To my father, who went home in 2024, thank you for teaching me steadiness, integrity, and quiet strength. As your eldest daughter, I will carry what you entrusted. Your mantle rests gently yet firmly on my shoulders.

I pray I honor it well.

Acknowledgments

This book was written during a time of global uncertainty marked by economic instability, technological acceleration, and spiritual confusion.

I am deeply grateful for:

My family, whose love strengthens my resolve.

Fellow believers who refuse to compromise truth for convenience.

Those working quietly within financial systems who understand both their power and their fragility.

Most of all, I acknowledge Jesus Christ, King above every system, authority above every government, and Lord over every currency.

Any clarity found within these pages comes from Him.

About the Author

Laura Lindsey brings over 20 years of experience in the banking industry, including 15 years specializing in Financial Crimes compliance. Her work in regulatory oversight, sanctions, fraud prevention, and risk management has given her a well informed understanding of the complexities of today's financial systems and the global forces influencing economic change.

Throughout her career, Laura has approached her role with a deep sense of responsibility to humbly serve and protect customers while supporting institutional integrity and sound risk practices. She believes God has been faithful in ordering her steps and that her professional journey has strengthened both her discernment and her confidence in her intuition and insight.

Grounded in a lifelong foundation of faith, Laura was raised in church by parents who served as youth leaders. She later spent 3 years serving on a deliverance ministry team. Her spiritual journey has shaped both her worldview and her professional path.

In *Death of the Dollar*, Laura brings together her financial expertise and Christian convictions to examine economic change through a biblical lens. She writes with clarity, balance, and hope, encouraging readers to remain spiritually attentive while trusting in God's faithfulness.

Married for 17 years, Laura and her husband cherish their blended family of 3 children, 3 grandchildren, with 1 on the way, and 3 bonus grandchildren. Above all, Laura is committed to leaving a legacy of faith and courage for generations to come.

Introduction
The Shaking Has Begun

Something is shifting.

It is not just about normal market ups and downs. It is not only about elections or political fights. It is not limited to headlines about inflation or interest rates. It is not simply about new technology moving forward. Something deeper is happening beneath what we see on the surface.

The foundation of the global financial system is moving.

For many years, the United States dollar has stood at the center of world trade. Oil has been priced in dollars. Countries have stored their national reserves in dollars. International business deals have depended on it. The dollar has not only been money. It has been a symbol of stability and power in a world that is often uncertain.

But even strong foundations can shift.

The United States dollar, once trusted without question, is now under pressure. Nations are buying large amounts of gold. Some countries are reducing their holdings of United States government debt. New trade deals are being made without using the dollar. Digital payment systems are growing quickly. Artificial intelligence is being built into financial monitoring systems. Central banks are testing digital currencies that can control how and when money is used.

Each of these changes may seem small on its own. Experts may argue about how important they are. Some may say they are normal adjustments in a changing economy.

But together they point to something bigger.

They point to transition.

Major changes rarely come with loud announcements. Most of the time, they are only clear after they have already happened. What feels like separate events may later be understood as the early stages of a large shift. The present moment shows many signs of such a shift.

This book is not an attempt to predict the future of markets. It is not written to guess exchange rates or forecast economic crashes. It is not financial advice.

It is a prophetic lens.

The Bible warns that in the last days systems will come together under stronger global authority. It speaks of a time when economic activity will be controlled and access to buying and selling will not be open to everyone. For many years, people saw these verses as symbolic or far away in the future. The images in Revelation and Daniel were often treated as spiritual ideas, not practical possibilities.

Today, the structure needed for such control exists.

Artificial intelligence can monitor activity.

Digital currency can limit or allow transactions.

Global cooperation can coordinate policy.

And crisis can push people to accept change.

Technology itself is not evil. Government itself is not automatically oppressive. Economic reform does not always mean prophecy is being fulfilled. But when monitoring power, financial control, global cooperation, and crisis come together in one system, the possibility of large scale control becomes real in a way it has never been before.

In past generations, a worldwide system that controlled buying and selling would have been impossible. Communication was too slow. Identification systems were weak. Enforcement was local, not global. There was no way to track and control everyone at the same time.

That is no longer true.

Biometric identification systems are already being used in many nations. Digital wallets can be turned on or off from a distance. Artificial intelligence can detect patterns and flag people within seconds. Financial transactions can be watched continuously. Banks across borders already work closely together.

The tools now exist.

This means the death of the dollar must be seen in a larger picture. It is not only about a weaker currency. It is not just about losing reserve status. It could become a turning point that speeds up global consolidation.

When money systems become unstable, people demand solutions. When fear spreads, leaders promise reform. Reform often leads to more central control. When central control joins with powerful technology, the ability to enforce rules grows stronger.

Economic instability can open the door to major restructuring.

History shows this pattern clearly. After world wars, international organizations were formed in the name of peace. After financial collapses, new regulations were put in place to prevent future crises. Each crisis led to new structures meant to bring stability.

Many of those structures were helpful.

But stability always has a cost.

When safety becomes the highest goal, freedom can slowly shrink. When efficiency becomes the focus, disagreement can be treated as disruption. When security becomes urgent, participation can depend on compliance.

The Bible describes a time when buying and selling will require authorization. It speaks of a period when economic participation will show where a person stands in loyalty. For many years, people struggled to imagine how such a system could exist on a global scale.

Now it is possible.

Artificial intelligence can analyze billions of transactions in real time. Digital currencies can be programmed with rules. Access can be tied to identity, location, or behavior. Digital identification systems can connect financial access, travel permission, communication, and health records under one profile.

The pieces are already in place.

This does not mean every new invention fulfills prophecy. It does not mean every recession signals the immediate end. Wisdom requires caution. But it is also unwise to ignore when the structure described in Scripture becomes technically possible.

When what the Bible describes can now be built, believers should pay attention.

The weakening of the dollar may be one of the early pains before a new economic system is born. Birth pains do not mean everything is ending. They mean something new is coming. They increase as the moment approaches.

In Matthew 24, Jesus spoke of wars, famines, and turmoil as the beginning of birth pains. Economic trouble fits into that pattern. Shaking is not random. It prepares the way for change.

Right now feels like early contraction.

Inflation reduces what money can buy.

War has historically been linked to inflation. Conflict disrupts production. It damages infrastructure. It increases government spending. It strains national debt. When wars involve key trade regions, the economic impact spreads quickly.

Ongoing tensions in the Middle East are especially significant because of critical shipping lanes that move oil and goods across continents. If those routes are threatened or restricted, trade slows. Energy prices rise. Supply chains tighten. Inflation follows.

These pressures may not be immediate. But they build over time. And when combined with existing financial strain, they intensify instability.

Supply chains struggle. Energy markets shift. Trade relationships change. Trust in governments and institutions weakens. At the same time, digital systems expand quickly, often presented as improvements and upgrades.

Fear grows during uncertain times.

When people are afraid, they look for strong solutions. They accept coordination. They welcome oversight. They may give up some freedom for the promise of stability.

Systems will always evolve. That is not the question. The real question is whether future systems will demand loyalty that conflicts with loyalty to Christ.

This book is not written in fear.

It is written from the view of a Christian warrior.

A warrior does not panic when shaking begins. Panic weakens judgment. A warrior studies the situation. A warrior prepares. Preparation is not fear. It is wisdom.

The Christian warrior understands that earthly kingdoms rise and fall. Empires grow and collapse. Currencies strengthen and weaken. None of this removes God from His throne. The Kingdom of God does not shake.

But we are still called to discern.

We are told to watch. We are told to understand the times. We are told to stay faithful, even when it costs us something. If one day economic participation depends on agreement with values that oppose Christ, that decision cannot be made in panic. It must already be settled in the heart.

This is not a call to hide from society. Believers are not called to withdraw from the world. We are called to live faithfully within it. But living faithfully requires clarity.

Clarity begins by recognizing transition.

If the dollar weakens and its global role shrinks, something else will rise to fill the gap. Power vacuums do not stay empty. New coalitions may form. Digital currencies may expand. Technology may take a greater role in oversight.

Structure shapes behavior.

When access to money is controlled by programmable systems, behavior can be rewarded or restricted. When identity is centralized, access can be granted or removed. When compliance is measured by algorithms, exclusion can happen instantly.

In the end, the deepest issue will not be technology. It will not be money. It will not even be politics.

It will be worship.

Behind every system stands a question of loyalty. The Bible makes clear that allegiance belongs to God alone. When participation in society becomes a sign of allegiance to something else, the line becomes clear.

This book does not set dates. It does not offer dramatic predictions. It looks at the direction of change through a biblical lens. It calls for preparation rooted in faith, not fear.

The shaking has begun.

Whether it increases slowly or suddenly is not yet known. What matters is that believers remain steady when systems tremble.

When systems begin to demand allegiance, you must already know where yours stands.

Matthew 24:6 to 8, KJV

"And ye shall hear of wars and rumours of wars: see that ye be not troubled: for all these things must come to pass, but the end is not yet.

For nation shall rise against nation, and kingdom against kingdom: and there shall be famines, and pestilences, and earthquakes, in divers places.

All these are the beginning of sorrows."

Chapter 1
The Illusion of Stability

For decades, the United States dollar has functioned as the backbone of global commerce. It has been the currency most nations trust. It has been the standard by which oil is priced, trade is settled, and reserves are stored. When countries do business with one another, the dollar has often stood in the middle of the transaction.

Because of this role, the dollar has come to represent more than money. It has represented security. It has represented influence. It has represented dominance.

When markets were unstable, investors ran to the dollar. When nations faced crisis, they stored their wealth in dollar based assets. When businesses needed stability, they trusted the system built around it. For many people, the dollar felt permanent. It felt unshakable.

But no earthly system is eternal.

History proves this again and again. Great empires have risen and fallen. Powerful governments have collapsed. Strong currencies have lost value and faded from global use. Rome once controlled trade across continents. The British pound once ruled global markets. Before that, other powers believed their strength would last forever.

None of them did.

Yet each generation tends to believe that its own system will endure. When something functions for a long time, people assume it will continue. Stability becomes normal. Normal becomes expected. Expected becomes trusted.

That trust forms what we can call an illusion of stability.

An illusion of stability does not mean the system is fake. It means people forget it can change. They stop imagining that it could weaken. They stop preparing for transition. They assume tomorrow will look like yesterday.

For many years, that assumption seemed reasonable. The dollar was strong. The United States economy was large. Military power supported financial power. Global trade relied on American banking systems. Confidence was high.

But stability is often strongest just before change.

Today we see signs that confidence is shifting. Nations are buying gold in large amounts. Some countries are reducing their holdings of United States Treasuries. Trade agreements are forming that bypass the dollar. Digital payment systems are expanding quickly. Central banks are testing their own digital currencies.

Each of these actions may appear technical or minor on its own. But together they suggest something deeper. They suggest repositioning. They suggest preparation for a different structure.

The weakening of the dollar is not just fiscal policy. It is not only about interest rates or debt ceilings. It signals that the architecture of global finance is shifting.

Architecture matters.

Architecture determines how a system functions. It determines who holds influence. It determines how control flows and how access is granted. When architecture changes, behavior changes. Power shifts. Authority moves.

For decades, the dollar has stood at the center of that architecture. If the center weakens, the entire structure must adjust.

This does not mean the dollar disappears overnight. Transitions rarely happen that way. They unfold in stages. They build through trends. They move through pressure and response.

The question is not whether the dollar will vanish tomorrow. The question is whether we are entering a season of structural change.

Scripture gives us a pattern for understanding such seasons.

In Matthew 24, Jesus warned that the last days would be marked by global shaking. He spoke of wars. He spoke of famines. He spoke of distress among nations. He described these events as "birth pains."

Birth pains do not signal extinction.

They signal transition.

When a mother feels birth pains, something is ending, but something else is beginning. The pain is not meaningless. It has purpose. It signals that a new stage is coming.

Jesus did not describe a calm and steady progression toward the end of the age. He described shaking. He described instability. He described pressure that increases before fulfillment.

Economic distress is part of that picture.

Money touches every part of life. It affects food, housing, trade, employment, and security. When economies shake, societies feel it deeply. Fear rises quickly when people worry about access to resources.

If we look at the world today, we see many forms of shaking. Wars continue in different regions. Supply chains have faced disruption. Inflation has reduced purchasing power in many countries. Trust in institutions has weakened. Political divisions have deepened.

These events are not isolated. They interact with one another. Economic weakness makes political tension worse. Political tension disrupts trade. Trade disruption increases financial strain. Financial strain increases public fear.

This is how birth pains operate. They increase in frequency and intensity.

The weakening of the dollar must be viewed within this larger pattern. It is not simply about one nation's policy choices. It is part of a global environment where confidence is shifting.

Confidence is the foundation of any currency.

Money has value because people believe it does. When trust is strong, a currency stands firm. When trust weakens, cracks begin to form.

For many years, trust in the dollar has been reinforced by habit and by necessity. Nations needed it for trade. Investors needed it for security. Systems were built around it.

But systems can be rebuilt.

New payment networks are emerging. Digital currencies offer alternatives to traditional banking rails. Regional alliances are exploring ways to settle trade without relying on the dollar. These changes do not yet remove the dollar from its position, but they reduce exclusive dependence on it.

Reduction of dependence is the first stage of transition.

When dependence decreases, influence decreases. When influence decreases, leverage weakens. When leverage weakens, the structure must adjust.

This adjustment can create instability. And instability often invites consolidation.

When systems shake, leaders promise solutions. When markets tremble, institutions offer reform. When fear spreads, coordination increases. People accept stronger oversight if it promises stability.

This is not new. It is human nature. In times of uncertainty, security becomes the highest priority.

But believers must look beyond the surface of events.

Jesus did not tell His followers to panic at signs of shaking. He told them to watch. He told them to understand the season. He told them that these birth pains would come.

The illusion of stability fades when shaking begins.

Recent public statements often describe the economy as strong. Officials point to lower gas prices, increased foreign investment, and new tariff strategies that are said to protect domestic industry. On the surface, these reports can create reassurance. They suggest growth. They suggest recovery. They suggest strength.

But surface improvement does not always mean structural stability.

Tariffs, for example, may encourage foreign investment in some sectors. Yet they also require American business owners to carry much of the upfront cost when purchasing goods from overseas. Those added expenses do not disappear. They move through the supply chain. They affect pricing. They affect margins. They increase financial strain on small and medium sized businesses.

Optimistic messaging can calm markets for a season. It can steady public emotion. But calm headlines do not always reflect deeper economic pressure.

Sometimes what appears to be peace is simply pause.

Scripture warns that there will be a time when people say, "Peace and safety," yet sudden disruption follows. A sense of improvement can create comfort. Comfort can reduce vigilance. And reduced vigilance can leave nations unprepared for deeper shifts already in motion.

What once felt permanent now feels uncertain. What once seemed secure now feels fragile.

That realization can produce fear.

But it can also produce clarity.

If no earthly system is eternal, then our trust must not rest in systems. If currencies rise and fall, then our security must not depend solely on them. If global finance can shift, then our foundation must be deeper than financial architecture.

This does not mean we ignore economic realities. It means we understand them in proper perspective.

The dollar has played a powerful role in modern history. It has shaped trade, policy, and influence. Its potential weakening matters. It will affect markets and nations. It may accelerate broader structural change.

But it is still part of an earthly system.

Earthly systems are temporary.

Scripture reminds us that only the Kingdom of God is unshaken. Every other structure, no matter how strong, exists within time. And what exists within time can be altered.

The illusion of stability is dangerous because it lulls people into complacency. It convinces them that preparation is unnecessary. It persuades them that change is unlikely.

Yet history and prophecy both warn otherwise.

We are entering a period where financial structures may be redefined. The weakening of the dollar is not an isolated event. It is part of a broader realignment of power, technology, and governance.

Birth pains signal that something new is forming.

The key question is not only what is ending, but what is beginning.

If global finance shifts away from a single dominant reserve currency, what replaces it? If trust in one system weakens, what new structure gains strength? If instability grows, who offers the solution?

These are not merely economic questions. They are spiritual ones.

The illusion of stability is fading. The shaking has begun. And when foundations move, wise builders examine where they stand.

Chapter 2
Gold, Treasuries, and the Quiet Realignment

The global financial system does not change in loud moments alone.

Often, it shifts quietly.

There are no dramatic announcements. No sudden declarations that the old system is ending. Instead, there are steady adjustments. Strategic decisions. Careful repositioning.

Right now, those quiet adjustments are taking place.

Nations are increasing gold reserves.

Foreign powers are reducing reliance on United States Treasuries.

Digital payment systems are expanding at a rapid pace.

These are not isolated financial trends.

They are structural repositioning.

To understand what this means, we must look at each piece carefully.

The Return to Gold

For many years, gold was viewed as old fashioned. Modern economies moved toward complex financial instruments, digital transactions, and paper assets backed by government trust. Gold remained valuable, but it did not sit at the center of daily economic discussion.

That has changed.

In recent years, central banks across the world have increased their gold purchases. Not in small amounts, but in record levels. Nations that once relied heavily on dollar based reserves are now diversifying. They are adding physical gold to their holdings.

Why?

Gold carries no counterparty risk. It is not a promise issued by another nation. It is not dependent on digital systems. It does not require political agreement. It is tangible. It is limited. It has held value for thousands of years.

When countries buy gold, they are not simply investing. They are protecting themselves against uncertainty.

Gold functions as a hedge against instability. It protects against inflation. It protects against currency devaluation. It protects against geopolitical risk.

When many nations increase gold reserves at the same time, it signals caution. It signals preparation. It signals reduced confidence in the current structure.

This does not mean gold will replace modern currency tomorrow. It does mean nations are building alternatives.

Gold is not a step backward. It is a stabilizer during transition.

The Treasury Question

For decades, United States Treasuries have been considered one of the safest assets in the world. Foreign governments bought them in large quantities. They stored national wealth in American debt. They trusted the stability of the dollar and the strength of the American economy.

That pattern is shifting.

Several major foreign holders have reduced their Treasury positions. Some are doing so gradually. Others are more direct. While not abandoning the system entirely, they are lowering exposure.

This matters because Treasuries are deeply connected to the dollar's role as a reserve currency. When foreign nations buy American debt, they strengthen the dollar's global position. When they reduce purchases, they weaken that support.

Again, this is not collapse. It is repositioning.

Countries are asking important questions. What happens if sanctions increase? What happens if geopolitical tensions rise? What happens if trade fragmentation grows? What happens if the dollar weakens long term?

Diversification is the response.

When reliance decreases, leverage decreases. When leverage decreases, power balances begin to shift.

This is how global architecture changes. Not through dramatic announcements, but through steady realignment.

The Rise of Digital Systems

While gold purchases increase and Treasury reliance adjusts, another force is accelerating.

Digital payment systems are expanding quickly.

Cash usage is declining in many nations. Mobile payments are becoming standard. Central banks are testing digital currencies. Financial technology companies are creating platforms that move money instantly across borders.

Speed is becoming the new normal.

Digital systems promise efficiency. They reduce transaction time. They increase transparency. They lower some operational costs. They make global commerce easier.

But digital systems also increase oversight.

Every digital transaction leaves a record. Every digital wallet can be tracked. Every digital system can be monitored.

This is not necessarily negative. Transparency can reduce fraud. Monitoring can improve compliance. Efficiency can help economic growth.

But it also changes control.

Cash allows anonymity. Digital systems reduce it.

When entire economies move toward digital platforms, financial access becomes dependent on infrastructure. Infrastructure requires governance. Governance requires policy.

The more digital the system becomes, the more centralized its oversight can become.

Patterns, Not Coincidences

Gold accumulation.

Reduced Treasury reliance.

Digital acceleration.

These are not random events.

They are responses to the same underlying pressure.

Trust in long term dollar dominance is being reassessed.

This does not mean the dollar has failed. It means nations are preparing for multiple outcomes. They are reducing dependence on a single center of gravity.

When many actors reposition at once, a quiet realignment is underway.

Realignment does not require panic. It requires awareness.

What Happens When Confidence Shifts

A reserve currency holds power because of confidence.

Countries use it because they trust its stability. Businesses price goods in it because they trust its acceptance. Investors store wealth in it because they trust its resilience.

When confidence weakens, change begins.

History shows that reserve currency transitions are rarely smooth. They take years. Sometimes decades. But they reshape global influence.

When one system weakens, the world does not return to barter. It does not scatter into chaos for long. It seeks a new center.

Markets demand order. Trade requires coordination. Governments seek stability.

The instinct during uncertainty is consolidation.

When confidence in a reserve currency wanes, centralization often follows.

Centralization as Response

Financial instability creates fear. Fear creates demand for solutions. Solutions often involve coordination at higher levels.

Regional alliances strengthen. International institutions gain influence. Standards become unified. Rules become harmonized.

Coordination can be beneficial. It can reduce volatility. It can prevent conflict. It can stabilize trade.

But coordination also concentrates authority.

When multiple nations align financial policy, the center grows stronger. When digital systems are integrated across borders, oversight becomes more unified.

The quiet realignment we are witnessing is not fragmentation alone. It is preparation for consolidation.

Gold provides security outside the system.

Reduced Treasury reliance reduces vulnerability to one nation.

Digital systems create new frameworks for coordination.

Together, they build the foundation for a different architecture.

The Illusion of Independence

Some may assume that diversification means decentralization. That nations pulling back from dollar reliance signals a move toward independence.

In the short term, that may appear true.

But global trade is too interconnected to operate without structure. Supply chains stretch across continents. Energy markets link nations together. Digital networks connect banks instantly.

Complete independence is unrealistic.

As dependence on one center decreases, coordination between multiple centers increases.

That coordination can eventually create a broader, more unified framework.

Realignment often moves from single dominance to shared governance, and shared governance often leads to centralized standards.

Technology Changes the Outcome

In past centuries, reserve transitions were slower and less integrated. Communication was limited.

Enforcement was local. Policy coordination took time.

Today, digital infrastructure changes that reality.

If a new financial framework emerges, it can be implemented rapidly. Systems can update instantly. Regulations can be embedded in software. Compliance can be automated.

Technology removes many of the delays that once slowed global change.

This is why digital acceleration matters alongside gold accumulation and Treasury reduction.

It shows preparation on two levels.

Physical security through gold.

Digital infrastructure for coordination.

One protects from instability.

The other enables restructuring.

Scripture and Structural Change

The Bible describes a time when economic participation will require authorization. It speaks of systems that influence buying and selling. It warns of consolidation under global authority.

For centuries, such control seemed impossible on a worldwide scale.

Today, it is technically feasible.

This does not mean every financial shift fulfills prophecy immediately. It does mean the conditions described in Scripture are no longer difficult to imagine.

When economic systems centralize, access becomes conditional.

When digital oversight expands, compliance becomes measurable.

When governance aligns across borders, enforcement becomes scalable.

The quiet realignment we see today may not yet be the final system. But it moves in that direction.

Preparing Without Panic

None of these developments require fear.

Transitions are part of history. Financial systems evolve. Nations adjust. Technology advances.

But awareness is necessary.

If the dollar's dominance weakens over time, the replacement will shape global behavior. If centralization increases, participation may carry new requirements.

Believers must understand these trends not to speculate wildly, but to discern wisely.

Gold purchases, Treasury adjustments, and digital acceleration are signals.

They tell us that the world is preparing for change.

The question is not whether change will come. Change is constant.

The question is what form the next structure will take.

The Direction of Movement

When confidence in reserve currency wanes, the world does not return to barter.

It centralizes.

It seeks stronger coordination.

It seeks unified standards.

It seeks stability through oversight.

The quiet realignment taking place today suggests that nations understand the current system may not remain unchanged forever.

Gold protects against instability.

Reduced Treasury exposure limits vulnerability.

Digital systems prepare for coordinated restructuring.

Together, they reveal movement.

The foundation is adjusting.

And when foundations adjust, wise observers pay attention.

Not with fear.

Not with anger.

But with discernment.

Because when structures shift quietly, the outcome is often decided long before the public fully recognizes the change.

The realignment is not loud.

It is steady.

And steady change reshapes the world.

Revelation 13:16 to 17, King James Version

"And he causeth all, both small and great, rich and poor, free and bond, to receive a mark in their right hand, or in their foreheads:

Chapter 3
Artificial Intelligence
The Nervous System
of the New Economy

Technology is not evil. It is a tool created and used by people. Like any tool, it reflects the intentions of those who design it and control it. A tool can be used to build, protect, and improve life. The same tool can also be used to restrict, monitor, or harm. The difference is not in the tool itself, but in the purpose behind it.

Throughout history, technology has improved daily life. It has helped doctors diagnose illness. It has helped farmers grow more food. It has allowed businesses to move goods across the world. It has connected families across long distances. Few would argue that all technology is dangerous. Most of it begins with a problem that someone wants to solve.

Artificial intelligence is no different in that sense. It is designed to process large amounts of information quickly. It can detect patterns. It can identify fraud. It can help companies predict supply shortages. It can support medical research. It can improve customer service. In many cases, it saves time and reduces human error.

These benefits are real and should be acknowledged.

But technology never exists on its own. It always operates within a system. Every system has leadership. Every system has rules. Every system has goals. Artificial intelligence does not act independently. It follows instructions. It applies standards. It enforces policies that are programmed into it.

That is why the central issue is not whether artificial intelligence is good or bad. The real issue is who controls it and how centralized that control becomes.

Centralized technology magnifies power because it removes barriers between decision and action. In earlier systems, authority moved slowly. If a government created a rule, local offices had to interpret and enforce it. If a bank restricted an account, a person could often speak to a manager. Delays existed. Human judgment existed. Alternatives often existed.

Artificial intelligence changes that structure. It allows decisions to be made instantly and at scale. It can review millions of transactions in seconds. It can compare behavior against preset rules. It can flag accounts automatically. It can limit access without waiting for human review.

When this ability is spread across many independent systems, its impact is limited. When it is centralized, its impact becomes much greater.

Centralization means fewer independent checkpoints. It means fewer alternatives. It means that one decision can carry across multiple systems at once. A single rule can affect banking, travel, employment, and communication if those systems are connected.

Artificial intelligence increases the speed and reach of enforcement. It does not need to sleep. It does not get tired. It does not overlook patterns. It does not hesitate. It simply follows instructions.

This is what makes it powerful.

Many people assume that control must appear harsh or visible. They imagine open force or public punishment. Modern control rarely begins that way. It often begins with efficiency. It begins with convenience. It begins with systems that promise safety and order.

Artificial intelligence fits naturally into that promise. It can reduce fraud. It can prevent cyber attacks. It can identify financial crime. It can improve regulatory compliance. Governments and financial institutions present it as a way to protect the public and strengthen stability.

There is truth in that. Financial systems are complex. Fraud and cyber threats are real. Monitoring tools can reduce harm.

The concern arises when monitoring becomes continuous and centralized. Cash transactions once allowed privacy. Paper systems limited the ability to track every detail of a person's activity. Digital systems remove much of that privacy. Artificial intelligence amplifies that removal.

Every digital transaction leaves a record. Artificial intelligence can analyze those records instantly. It can build behavior profiles. It can score risk. It can trigger automatic responses.

If financial access depends on digital systems, and digital systems depend on artificial intelligence, then participation in the economy becomes linked to algorithmic evaluation.

This does not mean every system will become oppressive. It means the potential exists in a way it did not before.

To understand the scale of this shift, consider how the human body functions. The body has organs that perform specific tasks. The heart pumps blood. The lungs bring in oxygen. The muscles create movement. But the nervous system connects everything. It carries signals. It sends warnings. It coordinates response. Without it, the body cannot act as a unified whole.

Artificial intelligence is becoming the nervous system of the modern economy. It connects banks, payment platforms, identity verification systems, and regulatory agencies. It carries information between them. It signals risk. It coordinates response.

If one part of the system detects a problem, artificial intelligence can communicate that instantly to other connected systems. A flagged transaction can lead to a restricted account. A restricted account can affect payment access. Payment access can affect employment or business activity.

The speed of this process is what changes the landscape.

In earlier times, enforcement required layers of review. Appeals could be made. Time existed between accusation and consequence. As systems centralize and automate, that time shrinks.

Automation also reduces human discretion. A programmed rule does not consider context unless it has been designed to do so. It does not weigh personal circumstances unless it has been instructed to. It does not pause to reflect.

When rules are fair and transparent, automation can improve consistency. When rules are unclear or politically influenced, automation can spread those rules quickly and widely.

Centralized artificial intelligence magnifies both the strengths and weaknesses of the system behind it.

Another important shift is the merging of identity and finance. Digital identity systems are expanding in many parts of the world. They link personal data with financial access. Artificial intelligence can verify identity through biometrics, track usage patterns, and detect irregularities.

This integration increases convenience. It also increases dependence.

If identity verification is required for every transaction, and artificial intelligence manages that verification, then participation becomes conditional on system approval. Access is no longer assumed. It is granted.

This is where the conversation moves beyond technology and into power.

Power grows when it becomes easier to enforce rules across large populations. Artificial intelligence provides that ease. It reduces the cost of monitoring. It reduces the time required to act. It reduces the number of human intermediaries needed.

When monitoring and enforcement become inexpensive and automatic, the temptation to expand them increases.

Again, the technology itself is not the enemy. Many developers build systems with good intentions. Many leaders want efficiency and safety. But history shows that centralized power, when left unchecked, can move beyond its original purpose.

The danger of centralized artificial intelligence is not that it appears cruel. It often appears helpful. It appears modern. It appears responsible.

It promises order in chaotic times.

In an era of financial instability, cyber threats, and global tension, such promises are attractive. People welcome systems that reduce risk. They accept oversight in exchange for stability.

This is why understanding artificial intelligence is essential to understanding the future of economic systems. It is not simply a tool that speeds up transactions. It is a system that can oversee, evaluate, and restrict participation at scale.

When connected to digital currency and centralized governance, artificial intelligence becomes the coordinating force that makes large scale enforcement practical.

The question for believers is not whether technology should be rejected. It is whether we recognize how power expands when systems merge and centralize.

Artificial intelligence is not the prophecy. It is the infrastructure that could support it.

As we move forward, we must examine how this nervous system of the new economy interacts with digital currency, compliance standards, and global coordination. Because when technology, finance, and authority connect under centralized oversight, participation in society can become more than economic.

It can become conditional.

The Expanding Capabilities of Artificial Intelligence

Artificial intelligence is no longer limited to research labs or experimental software. It is already embedded in modern financial systems. Banks use it. Governments use it. Payment platforms rely on it. It operates quietly in the background of daily transactions.

Its role continues to expand.

One of its most powerful abilities is real time transaction monitoring. Every time money moves digitally, a record is created. Artificial intelligence can scan millions of these records instantly. It looks for patterns. It detects unusual behavior. It flags transactions that do not match expected activity.

In earlier systems, monitoring required teams of people reviewing reports after the fact. Today, review happens immediately. A transaction can be evaluated the moment it occurs. If it triggers a preset rule, action can follow within seconds.

This speed changes the nature of financial oversight.

Artificial intelligence also enables predictive risk modeling. It does not only look at what has happened. It attempts to predict what might happen next. By analyzing past behavior, spending habits, location data, and account history, it can generate risk scores. These scores influence decisions.

A person or business may never see this score. Yet it can affect access to loans, payment approvals, or account status. Risk assessment becomes automated. Judgment becomes numerical.

In addition to monitoring and prediction, artificial intelligence supports automated sanctions. If a rule is violated, the response does not always require a human decision. Systems can freeze funds, restrict transfers, or block transactions automatically.

This can prevent fraud. It can stop illegal activity. But it also reduces the gap between suspicion and consequence. A flagged account can become a restricted account almost instantly.

Another major development is biometric digital identity. Many financial systems now use fingerprints, facial recognition, or other biometric data to verify identity. Artificial intelligence compares live scans to stored records. It determines whether access should be granted.

Biometric systems increase security. They also connect identity directly to financial access. When identity becomes fully digital and centralized, it becomes the key to participation.

The final capability is instant financial exclusion. If artificial intelligence determines that an account violates policy, access can be suspended immediately. Digital wallets can be disabled. Payment privileges can be withdrawn. Transfers can be blocked.

This process does not require physical force. It does not require visible confrontation. It happens within software.

Taken individually, each of these tools can serve legitimate purposes. Monitoring reduces crime. Risk modeling protects institutions. Sanctions enforce rules. Identity systems prevent fraud.

But together, they form a structure capable of broad control.

Revelation 13 describes a system in which no one may buy or sell without authorization. For centuries, many readers viewed this as symbolic language. The idea of a single structure controlling economic participation across the world seemed impossible.

There was no infrastructure to support it. There was no way to monitor all transactions. There was no unified system to verify identity globally. There was no technology capable of enforcing compliance at scale.

Today, the logistical barriers have largely disappeared.

Digital transactions are common across much of the world. Identity systems are becoming standardized. Financial institutions share information across borders. Artificial intelligence processes data in real time.

This does not mean that current systems are the final fulfillment of prophecy. It means that what once seemed unrealistic is now technically possible.

Artificial intelligence becomes the nervous system of a globalized economic body. It connects institutions. It carries signals between platforms. It evaluates behavior. It coordinates response.

Just as the nervous system allows the human body to react instantly to danger, artificial intelligence allows financial systems to respond instantly to perceived risk. If one part detects a violation, the information can spread across the network.

The body of the economy becomes unified in response.

Prophecy does not require technology to be fulfilled. Scripture was written long before modern systems existed. But technology now provides a mechanism through which large scale economic authorization can function smoothly and efficiently.

Total compliance does not require visible force when digital systems manage access. If buying and selling depend on digital approval, and digital approval depends on centralized standards evaluated by artificial intelligence, then compliance becomes measurable and enforceable.

Scalability is the key difference. In earlier eras, enforcing universal rules would have required physical oversight. Today, software can do it.

Artificial intelligence allows systems to grow without losing control. It allows oversight to expand without proportional increases in manpower. It allows enforcement to operate continuously.

This is why understanding artificial intelligence is essential. Not because it is evil, but because it magnifies whatever structure governs it.

If the structure is fair and limited, artificial intelligence can serve well. If the structure becomes controlling and demands allegiance, artificial intelligence can enforce that demand efficiently.

The capability now exists for economic participation to be conditional in ways that previous generations could not have imagined. That reality should not produce panic. It should produce awareness.

Awareness leads to discernment.

Discernment prepares the heart before the system ever demands a choice.

1 Thessalonians 5:3

"For when they shall say, Peace and safety; then sudden destruction cometh upon them, as travail upon a woman with child; and they shall not escape."

Chapter 4
The Board of Peace
Crisis as Catalyst

In the previous chapters, we discussed the growing instability in the global financial system. From the weakening of the dollar to the rise of digital currencies, the world is changing in ways that many are still trying to understand. This growing instability is not happening in isolation. It is part of a larger pattern of uncertainty and change affecting nations, economies, and industries. As this uncertainty grows, it is clear that the world is approaching a major turning point.

History teaches us that major crises often lead to the creation of new systems designed to bring stability. When chaos and disruption take over, people and nations look for ways to restore peace, rebuild, and prevent further damage. In these times, new organizations and councils are often formed to help manage the aftermath and guide the world back to order.

Now, as we look at today's world, we see a new set of challenges. Currency instability, cyber warfare, regional conflicts, and supply chain failures are all creating a perfect storm. These crises are linked together in ways that demand a global response. This chapter will explore how these problems are pushing the world toward a new kind of global organization — a Board of Peace — and what that could mean for the future of the world.

History Shows Us That Crisis Breeds Councils

Throughout history, some of the most important global organizations were formed in response to crisis. When the world is shaken by events like war or economic collapse, nations recognize the need for cooperation to rebuild and restore order. These crises push countries to come together, often creating new systems designed to prevent future chaos and bring stability to a fractured world.

For instance, after the devastation of World War II, leaders from around the world understood that the old systems could no longer prevent such widespread destruction. The United Nations was formed to encourage peace and cooperation between nations. Its mission was clear: prevent future wars and promote international cooperation on critical issues like human rights and global security.

Similarly, after the Great Depression, which caused widespread economic hardship, nations realized the global financial system needed stronger regulation. This led to the creation of the International Monetary Fund (IMF) and the World Bank, organizations designed to stabilize international economies and help countries in need of financial support. These institutions became crucial in managing the post-depression recovery.

Even during the Cold War, with tensions between the East and West, the world saw the formation of various alliances and peacekeeping organizations. The goal was to manage the growing risk of nuclear conflict and ensure that the world's superpowers could work together in some capacity, despite their differences.

While these organizations were established to bring stability, they were not without their challenges. While the UN, IMF, and World Bank helped create a more cooperative world, they also raised questions about the balance of power and the influence of stronger nations over weaker ones. For example, the UN's ability to maintain peace has often been questioned, especially when powerful nations use their veto power to block decisions.

In every case, the world responded to crisis by creating new systems that would attempt to restore peace and order. Yet, as history shows, the peace these councils aimed for often comes at a cost, one that may include loss of sovereignty or power, but also one that reflects the world's willingness to cooperate in the face of significant challenges.

A Perfect Storm: The Current Global Crisis

The world today is experiencing a perfect storm, where multiple crises are coming together at once. While these issues have been growing for some time, the weakening of the dollar has made their effects much worse. As the dollar becomes less stable, it starts a chain of events, creating uncertainty around the world.

The first crisis in this storm is the collapse of currencies. The US dollar, which has long been the world's main currency, is no longer as reliable as it once was. Countries are starting to lose confidence in it, and this uncertainty is spreading to other currencies. As nations look for alternatives, the global financial system faces the risk of breaking apart.

At the same time, there are signs that the banking system may be facing increasing pressure. As financial systems around the world experience strain, some observers believe banks could find it more challenging to maintain the same level of stability seen in previous decades. Rising debt levels, loan defaults, and growing concerns about the global economy have led many analysts to question whether the banking system will continue to provide the same sense of security people have long relied upon. While banks remain a central part of the financial system, these developments suggest that the system may be entering a period of greater uncertainty.

Cyber warfare is another growing threat. As economies and financial systems become more digital, they also become more vulnerable to attacks. Hackers are targeting everything from personal data to entire national systems. Cyber threats are no longer just an abstract problem they are causing real damage to markets, spreading panic, and destabilizing entire regions.

Regional conflicts are adding to the tension. Whether it's territorial disputes, political instability, or trade wars, these conflicts are creating more uncertainty. These disruptions affect global trade, supply chains, and even the stability of governments. The impact is felt far beyond the immediate region, as global markets are connected in ways that cause local problems to spread across the world.

Supply chain failures are also making things worse. The pandemic showed just how fragile global supply chains are, and even as the world recovers, problems continue. Shortages of essential goods, rising costs, and shipping delays are affecting industries everywhere. These problems are not only damaging economies but also shaking people's trust in the reliability of global systems.

Each of these crises is connected. The weakening of the dollar, for example, leads to inflation, which then causes problems in the banking system and fuels tensions in regional conflicts. Cyber attacks have an impact on trade and finance across borders. And the breakdown of supply chains only makes things worse, making it harder for countries to recover and stabilize.

The World Demands Coordination

As the world faces multiple crises at once, it is becoming clear that global coordination is no longer optional. Countries are increasingly recognizing that they cannot address these challenges alone. The interconnected nature of today's problems, such as currency instability, banking failures, cyber threats, and supply chain disruptions, means that solutions require cooperation on an international scale.

Nations are beginning to look for ways to unify their responses. They understand that isolated efforts will not be enough to restore stability. The idea of a "Board of Peace" has emerged as a potential solution. This multinational coalition would serve as a centralized body to address the ongoing crises and stabilize the global system. It would unite governments, businesses, and international organizations to create coordinated actions for financial recovery, peacekeeping, and economic regulation.

As the crises continue to deepen, the need for such an organization becomes more urgent. Governments are realizing that only through international cooperation can they hope to restore the balance and secure a more stable future. The world is moving toward a system where global institutions will play a central role in shaping responses to these challenges.

Promises of the Board of Peace

The idea of a Board of Peace promises a solution to the growing global instability. The coalition would focus on several key areas, each aiming to bring order and predictability back to the world's systems.

1. **Stabilizing Global Finance**

   One of the primary goals of the Board of Peace would be to stabilize global finance. With the dollar's decline and financial markets in turmoil, countries need to coordinate their economic policies to prevent further crashes. This would involve creating new regulations, ensuring financial institutions are better equipped to handle crises, and working together to keep the global economy functioning smoothly.

2. **Integrating Digital Currencies**

To modernize and streamline the global economy, the Board of Peace would integrate digital currencies into the financial system. Digital currencies could replace outdated systems, providing more efficient ways of conducting global transactions. They could help eliminate barriers to trade and finance, making the global market more inclusive and less dependent on traditional financial institutions.

3. **Preventing Economic Warfare**

As nations vie for economic power, there is growing concern about economic warfare, such as sanctions, tariffs, and trade restrictions. The Board of Peace could address this by creating rules and standards for international trade. By establishing clear guidelines and promoting fair practices, this body would work to prevent countries from using economic power as a weapon, fostering a more cooperative global economy.

4. **Using Artificial Intelligence to Forecast Instability**

Another major promise of the Board of Peace is the use of artificial intelligence (AI) to predict and manage global instability. AI could analyze vast amounts of data to spot emerging risks and forecast economic shifts before they occur. This would allow for proactive responses to crises, helping governments and businesses prepare for potential shocks before they hit.

5. **Overseeing Global Digital ID Systems**

The Board of Peace would also oversee the creation and management of global digital ID systems. These systems would help manage financial access, making transactions more secure and reducing fraud. By centralizing identity verification, the Board of Peace could ensure that only authorized individuals have access to critical financial resources, improving security in a rapidly digital world.

These goals seem rational and necessary in the context of the current instability. The idea of a global coalition working together to address these interconnected issues offers hope for a more coordinated and peaceful world. However, while these promises sound ideal, it is important to understand the potential costs involved.

The Board of Peace: Present Reality, Future Trajectory

A Board of Peace already exists today. Its stated mission focuses on stabilization, reconstruction, and coordination in regions affected by conflict. The language used by such institutions is usually careful and administrative. It speaks about rebuilding infrastructure, supporting recovery, and helping governments restore stability after crisis.

There is nothing prophetic about rebuilding cities or restoring services after war. These efforts are often necessary and can bring real relief to people who are suffering.

However, history shows that institutions formed during times of crisis often grow beyond their original purpose. Over time, their responsibilities expand. Oversight increases. Authority becomes more centralized. What begins as a temporary solution can gradually become a permanent structure.

Peace agreements often create the framework for cooperation. Economic systems then provide the mechanisms that enforce those frameworks.

Modern economies already operate through systems of authorization. Financial transactions require verification. Access to banking networks depends on compliance with regulations. Participation in global markets requires alignment with established rules. These systems were created to promote security, accountability, and transparency. In themselves, they are not the mark described in Revelation.

Yet Revelation 13 describes a future moment when economic authorization becomes something more than regulation. It becomes a test of allegiance. Buying and selling become tied not only to compliance with rules, but to loyalty to an authority that stands in opposition to Christ.

The technological infrastructure that could support such a system already exists. Digital payment networks operate in real time. Transactions can be approved or denied instantly. Access to financial systems can be granted or removed across borders with very little delay.

Infrastructure alone does not mean prophecy has been fulfilled. But it removes the barriers that once made such a system impossible.

Today, peace governance structures and economic authorization systems operate separately. Scripture suggests that a time may come when political authority and economic enforcement move together in a unified system.

Those who watch the times do not respond with panic. They pay attention to direction and trajectory.

Peace frameworks deserve careful observation. Not because peace itself is dangerous, but because throughout history, power has often consolidated under the promise of stability.

And history shows that systems created during seasons of crisis rarely disappear once the crisis has passed.

The Hidden Cost of Consolidation

While the promises of the Board of Peace may sound appealing, there are significant risks associated with global consolidation. The idea of one multinational coalition controlling global systems raises important questions about power, freedom, and control.

One of the major concerns is the potential loss of individual freedoms. A centralized body overseeing global finance, trade, and digital identities means that decisions about who gets access to resources, who controls the economy, and how information is shared could be made by a small group of powerful nations or corporations. As power becomes more centralized, the ability for nations or individuals to act independently becomes limited.

National sovereignty could also be at risk. Countries would have to give up some of their control over their own economic and political systems in exchange for the stability offered by a global coalition. While this may be necessary in times of crisis, it raises the question: at what cost do we gain stability?

The balance between security and freedom is delicate. On the one hand, global cooperation could lead to a more secure, stable world. On the other hand, it could result in a loss of personal freedom, economic autonomy, and political independence. The consolidation of power into a global system could create a world where individual nations have less say in their own future.

As we move toward this new global order, it is essential to think carefully about the trade-offs we are making. While the promise of peace and stability is appealing, we must ask ourselves what we are willing to sacrifice to achieve it.

The Need for Vigilance in Times of Global Uncertainty

As we navigate the growing global instability, it is important to remember the biblical warning found in **1 Thessalonians 5:3**, which states: *"When they say, 'Peace and safety,' then sudden destruction comes."* This verse serves as a reminder that appearances can be deceiving. While the idea of global coordination and a "Board of Peace" may seem like the solution to the crises we face, it's crucial to remain cautious. What may appear as peace and stability could, in reality, be a step toward a system that comes with unforeseen consequences.

The promises of global governance, whether through digital currencies, financial coordination, or AI-driven solutions, sound rational and necessary. However, we must not overlook the potential dangers. History has shown us that in times of crisis, powerful systems are often put in place that could limit freedom and sovereignty in exchange for perceived security.

In these uncertain times, it is essential for us to remain vigilant. We must think critically about the systems being created for global coordination. While cooperation between nations is important, we must ask ourselves: What are we willing to sacrifice for stability? Are we prepared for the consequences of a more centralized global system?

The challenges ahead will require wisdom, discernment, and a deep commitment to our values. As we face these interconnected crises, let us keep our eyes open, ensuring that the peace we seek is one that aligns with true justice and freedom. We must be aware of the systems being put in place and remain alert to the changes they bring, understanding that in times of crisis, the cost of peace can be much higher than we expect.

Daniel 7:23 (KJV)

"Thus he said, the fourth beast shall be the fourth kingdom upon earth, which shall be diverse from all kingdoms, and shall devour the whole earth, and shall tread it down, and break it in pieces."

Chapter 5
The Convergence of Control

As the world faces greater uncertainty and interconnected crises, the need for a new global system becomes clearer. The instability we are witnessing today is pushing nations toward a more unified approach to governance. This is where the concept of the "Convergence of Control" comes into play.

Three key pillars are forming the backbone of the system that will emerge to handle the world's growing challenges: digital currency, artificial intelligence, and centralized governance. Each of these pillars plays a crucial role in shaping the future of global control, but together, they create a system that can monitor, manage, and enforce participation across the globe.

Individually, these pillars are powerful tools. However, when combined, they offer a level of control and oversight that we have never seen before. They provide the foundation for a world where access to resources, services, and even participation in the economy depends on centralized approval.

As we move further into this new era, the question is not whether these systems will emerge, but how they will affect the freedoms we once took for granted. In the sections that follow, we will examine these three developments: digital currency, artificial intelligence, and centralized governance, and explore how their convergence could reshape the future of global economic participation.

Digital Currency: Economic Leverage in the New World Order

One of the most significant changes happening in the global economy is the rise of digital currencies. These currencies, which exist only in digital form, are quickly becoming a key tool for controlling the flow of money across the world. Unlike traditional money, digital currencies are not tied to physical assets like gold or silver. Instead, they are controlled by governments or large financial institutions, giving them the power to monitor and regulate transactions more easily.

Digital currencies provide governments and international organizations with the ability to track every transaction, from small purchases to large international trades. This kind of oversight offers many benefits, such as reducing fraud and making transactions more efficient. But it also means that the power to control economic participation lies in the hands of those who manage the digital currency system.

In a world where digital currencies are the standard, economic leverage becomes a powerful tool. Governments can easily restrict access to money, block transactions, or even freeze assets if individuals or businesses are deemed a threat or do not follow the rules. This level of control over financial systems can ensure stability, but it also raises concerns about privacy, freedom, and the potential for abuse of power.

The widespread use of digital currencies means that money, once seen as a private and personal matter, will become fully transparent. Governments and global organizations will have more control over how money flows, who gets access to it, and how it can be used. This shift represents a major change in the global financial landscape, as nations seek to ensure their economic stability in an increasingly uncertain world.

Artificial Intelligence: Technological Oversight and Control

As digital currencies are transforming the way money is handled, artificial intelligence (AI) is changing how the world manages everything from financial transactions to security and even governance. AI is no longer just a tool for research or entertainment; it is becoming an integral part of the global system of control.

AI is being used to monitor systems, predict risks, and make decisions in real-time. Governments and organizations are already using AI to track everything from market trends to personal behavior. With its ability to analyze vast amounts of data quickly, AI can spot patterns, forecast instability, and even manage responses to crises before they escalate.

In the convergence of control, AI plays a key role in overseeing global systems. By processing enormous amounts of data, AI can enforce rules, ensure compliance, and even predict future problems. For example, AI can monitor digital currency transactions to detect fraud or unusual behavior, providing quick solutions to prevent financial crises.

While AI has the potential to create a more efficient and secure system, it also presents significant challenges. Its ability to control systems in real-time means that decisions can be made without human intervention, which raises questions about accountability and transparency. Who decides how AI is used? And who is responsible when AI makes a mistake or is used to restrict freedoms?

AI's role in global governance is rapidly expanding, and with it, the reach of those who control the technology. In a world where AI is embedded in every aspect of society, it will not only monitor financial systems but also influence the way people live, work, and interact.

Centralized Governance: Political Authority in a Unified World

As digital currencies and artificial intelligence create new systems for economic and technological control, the third pillar of the convergence of control, centralized governance, ensures that these systems can be implemented effectively across the globe. In a world where interconnected crises require quick, coordinated responses, centralized governance provides the framework for political authority on a global scale.

Centralized governance means that power would no longer rest solely with individual nations. Instead, global institutions, such as multinational coalitions, international organizations, or even newly formed governing bodies, would hold decision-making authority. These bodies would be responsible for creating and enforcing global policies, setting standards for financial systems, and regulating industries that impact the world on a massive scale.

The idea of centralized governance offers the promise of efficiency. By pooling resources, expertise, and decision-making power, global institutions could respond more quickly to crises like economic instability, climate change, or pandemics. Coordination among nations could help avoid conflicts, ensure equitable resource distribution, and create solutions that benefit the entire planet.

However, the cost of such coordination is significant. As power becomes more centralized, individual nations may lose the ability to govern themselves freely. The political independence of countries could be compromised as decisions that once rested with national governments shift to international bodies. In a world where political authority is concentrated in the hands of a few global institutions, citizens may find their personal freedoms constrained by regulations and policies that they have no direct influence over.

The shift toward centralized governance raises important questions about the future of democracy, autonomy, and national sovereignty. While the promise of unity and stability may seem appealing in times of crisis, we must carefully consider the balance between security and freedom. As global power consolidates, we must ask ourselves: What price are we willing to pay for stability?

The Power of Convergence

The three pillars of the convergence of control are digital currency, artificial intelligence, and centralized governance. They are not isolated from each other. Instead, they work together to form a powerful system that offers both efficiency and control. Each pillar strengthens the others, creating a system that is greater than the sum of its parts.

Digital currencies provide the economic framework for global transactions, allowing for precise control over the flow of money and ensuring that financial systems are more transparent and regulated. Artificial intelligence acts as the overseer, analyzing vast amounts of data in real-time to predict risks and enforce rules. Meanwhile, centralized governance holds the political authority to make decisions, regulate actions, and ensure global coordination.

Individually, these pillars are strong, but when combined, they create a system where participation in the global economy and access to essential services becomes conditional. The ability to use digital currency, access certain technologies, or even move freely within the global system may depend on compliance with the rules set by centralized authorities.

If one of these pillars were removed or weakened, the enforcement system would become less effective. For example, without the structure of centralized governance, digital currencies would lack the regulatory framework needed for global coordination. Without artificial intelligence, it would be much harder to monitor and enforce compliance in real-time.

Together, these three pillars form a unified system that ensures global participation is tightly controlled. This system may appear efficient and necessary in times of crisis, but we must be cautious of the price we pay for this level of control. The interconnectedness makes it a powerful tool, but it also creates a future where freedom may be limited in exchange for stability.

The Mark: A New Form of Control

As the convergence of control grows stronger, discussions often return to the biblical warning found in Revelation, where participation in the economy or society is connected to a mark. In a modern world shaped by digital systems and identity verification, many observers wonder how such control could appear within advanced financial networks.

In the future, access to financial systems, services, and even basic rights may depend on forms of centralized authorization. Systems could verify identity and authorize transactions through digital means such as global digital identification, biometric authentication, or implantable technologies capable of functioning similarly to modern tap to pay systems, linking identity, authorization, and the ability to buy or sell within a single digital framework. In such a structure, access to money, resources, and even freedom of movement could be influenced by systems that grant or deny participation within financial networks.

The mark described in Revelation points to the ability to control who can and cannot participate in the global economy under the direction of the Antichrist. Advancing technology has made large scale monitoring possible. Digital identities and artificial intelligence systems are increasingly capable of tracking, monitoring, and evaluating transactions or activities across financial platforms.

While these systems are often presented as improvements in security and efficiency, they also introduce important questions. The power to grant or withhold access to resources becomes a form of authority that could be misused if concentrated in the wrong hands. Systems that regulate participation could eventually influence which behaviors, actions, or allegiances are considered acceptable.

Participation in future financial systems may increasingly depend on alignment with regulatory and digital frameworks. Whatever it is called in its day, its function will matter more than its label.

At this point it is also important to acknowledge an area where sincere believers hold different views. Many Christians believe the Church will be taken in a pre tribulation rapture before the events connected to the mark of the beast occur. Others believe the Church may experience periods of persecution before Christ returns. Scripture makes clear that allegiance to Christ must remain uncompromised regardless of the season.

Pre tribulation hope is comforting, but no one knows the exact time or day Christ will return. The New Testament repeatedly prepares believers for endurance, faithfulness, and perseverance under pressure. Jesus said, "He that endureth to the end shall be saved." (Matthew 24:13)

Whichever timeline one believes, the posture remains the same. Faithful. Watchful. Uncompromised.

Efficiency Over Brutality: The Beast System Begins

The system described in biblical prophecy may not appear in the way many people expect. It may not begin with violence, force, or obvious oppression. Instead, it may begin through systems designed to improve organization, coordination, and convenience. As the convergence of control develops under the control of the antichrist, digital currencies, artificial intelligence, and centralized governance may be introduced as tools intended to address global problems.

In such a system, financial transactions could occur instantly. Data could be analyzed in real time to detect risk or instability. Global coordination could help trade move more smoothly, while centralized governance might allow rapid responses to crises.

Convenience may play a large role in public acceptance. Digital currencies could make transactions faster and simpler. Artificial intelligence may offer predictions that help prevent instability. Centralized coordination could appear to strengthen international cooperation and stability.

Yet behind these benefits lies an important question about control. As more aspects of daily life become connected to digital systems, the ability to monitor, restrict, or regulate participation increases. Systems created to maintain order could also be used to enforce conformity.

At first, the power of such systems may appear subtle. Rather than immediate force, the system could shape behavior by limiting available choices. Participation in financial networks and services could depend on compliance with rules set by powerful institutions. Access to money, resources, or services could be granted or denied depending on behavior, loyalty, or compliance.

What begins as technological progress could gradually reshape how people interact with society. As reliance on these systems grows, choosing to live outside them may become increasingly difficult. Over time, systems created to provide stability could also become mechanisms that influence behavior and participation.

The Cost of Participation: Freedom or Security?

As we move further into this new system, it becomes clear that there will be significant trade-offs. The systems put in place to bring stability and order are not without their cost. The rise of digital currencies, artificial intelligence, and centralized governance promises a more organized and secure world. But these promises come at a price, a price that many may not fully realize until it is too late.

The most significant cost is the potential loss of freedom. As participation in the global system becomes conditioned on compliance with centralized rules, individual choices will become limited. Access to basic services, financial systems, and even personal freedoms may be determined by how well individuals follow the rules set by the global system. People may find themselves forced to comply with a set of standards they have no power to influence or change.

While security is a fundamental need, the question remains: How much are we willing to sacrifice in order to feel safe? When control over our economic participation, our ability to access services, and even our movement is placed in the hands of a few powerful institutions, the question of freedom versus security becomes even more pressing.

The systems of control will likely begin with the promise of greater convenience, faster transactions, and improved efficiency. These benefits will appeal to many. However, as these systems grow, they will gradually strip away the choices we once had. The more we rely on these systems, the less control we will have over our own lives.

In the end, the choice will be between security and autonomy. The world that is emerging will be one where safety and stability are prioritized above individual freedom. But as we accept these new systems, we must ask ourselves: At what point does security become a form of control? And what is the true cost of giving up our freedoms for the sake of stability?

The Path Toward a Conditional World

As we have explored throughout this chapter, the convergence of control represents a powerful new global system, one that is being built upon the pillars of digital currency, artificial intelligence, and centralized governance. These three pillars are rapidly coming together, forming a framework for a world where participation is no longer a universal right, but a conditional privilege.

In the face of growing global instability, these systems promise stability, efficiency, and security. However, the cost of these promises is steep. The more we rely on digital currencies and AI-driven governance, the more our freedoms are limited. Participation in the global economy will increasingly depend on compliance with rules set by powerful global institutions. The question we must all ask is: *What are we willing to sacrifice for the sake of stability?* Will we trade personal freedoms for security, and if so, at what cost?

As these systems of control take shape, it is essential to remain vigilant. What may seem like a solution to current crises may become a system of control that limits individual rights and choices. The future is uncertain, but one thing is clear: the path to a more coordinated world will not come without its trade-offs. The journey ahead requires careful thought and discernment, as we balance the desire for safety with the need to preserve freedom.

In the next chapter, we will explore a possible progression of events that aligns with biblical prophecy. From the early signs of monetary destabilization to the rise of a global economic system, we will walk through the stages that seem to be leading us toward the establishment of the Board of Peace and a new global order.

Revelation 18:17 (KJV)

"For in one hour so great riches is come to nought. And every shipmaster, and all the company in ships, and sailors, and as many as trade by sea, stood afar off."

Chapter 6
The Pattern
Scripture Reveals

Throughout Scripture there are moments when economic systems shift in ways that reshape entire societies. When these passages are examined together, they reveal a pattern that repeats across history. The Bible does not simply record spiritual events. It also describes how wealth, power, and control often move through recognizable stages.

This pattern becomes especially striking when viewed in light of modern economic discussions. The shifts taking place in global finance today may feel unprecedented, yet Scripture shows that systems of wealth and power have followed similar trajectories before.

When several passages are placed side by side, a four stage pattern begins to emerge.

Wealth Concentration During Crisis

One of the earliest examples appears in Genesis 47 during the severe famine in Egypt. Joseph, serving under Pharaoh, oversees the distribution of grain as the famine spreads across the region. As the crisis deepens, people begin exchanging what they have in order to survive.

First they bring their money to purchase grain. When their money is gone, they return with their livestock. As the famine continues, they eventually sell their land in exchange for food. Finally, many place themselves into servitude so that they can continue receiving provisions.

Within a short period of time, an enormous transfer of wealth and property takes place. Land, livestock, and labor all become centralized under the authority of Pharaoh.

The passage does not present this event as evil in itself. Joseph's actions preserve lives during a devastating famine. Yet the account provides a clear example of how crisis can accelerate the concentration of economic power. When survival is at stake, people often surrender resources and independence in exchange for stability.

Many economists today observe that major crises frequently produce similar outcomes. Financial stress, war, or widespread instability often lead to greater consolidation of wealth and authority.

Prosperity and Expanding Trade

Another stage appears during the reign of King Solomon. Under Solomon's leadership, Israel enters a period of remarkable prosperity and international trade. First Kings 10 describes the kingdom as a center of wealth and commerce, connected to distant regions through expanding trade routes.

Gold flows into the kingdom from many lands. Ships carry goods across seas. Merchants bring rare materials, precious metals, spices, and luxury items from far away nations. The text describes an economy that appears strong, prosperous, and deeply connected to global exchange.

This period stands as one of the clearest biblical descriptions of large scale international trade and economic abundance.

Yet the prosperity does not last indefinitely. After Solomon's reign, the kingdom fractures and the stability that once seemed secure begins to unravel. The wealth that symbolized strength proves more fragile than it first appeared.

Wealth Systems That Become Corrupt

The New Testament also addresses the moral dangers that can develop within economic systems. In James chapter five, believers are warned about wealth that becomes corrupted by injustice.

The passage speaks of riches that have been hoarded while workers are denied fair wages. It describes economic structures where power and wealth are used in ways that harm others and ignore righteousness.

James writes that such conditions will be present in the last days. His warning is not directed at money itself, but at systems that place wealth above justice and compassion.

Scripture consistently teaches that wealth is not inherently evil. Yet when economic systems begin to prioritize power and profit above righteousness, they become vulnerable to corruption.

The Collapse of a Global System

The final stage appears in Revelation 18, where a powerful commercial system known symbolically as Babylon suddenly falls. The chapter describes merchants, traders, and shipmasters mourning because the economic network that once sustained them has collapsed.

The passage lists cargoes of luxury goods, precious metals, spices, fabrics, and merchandise moving through global trade routes. It paints a picture of an extensive commercial system that appeared stable and prosperous.

Yet the collapse happens with shocking speed.

The phrase repeated throughout the chapter is striking. The fall occurs "in one hour." What seemed permanent proves fragile. A system that once dominated the world economy disappears suddenly, leaving merchants and traders stunned by its downfall.

The Pattern That Repeats

When these passages are viewed together, a recognizable sequence appears.

Economic systems often begin by centralizing power during periods of crisis. Stability follows as trade expands and prosperity grows. Over time, wealth systems can drift toward corruption when righteousness is replaced by the pursuit of power. Eventually the system collapses, often far more suddenly than anyone expected.

This pattern appears again and again across history.

Systems rise.

Wealth concentrates.

Corruption grows.

And eventually the system falls.

The Bible does not present these patterns merely as economic observations. They serve as reminders that human systems, no matter how powerful they appear, remain temporary.

No economic structure lasts forever. No system built by human authority remains permanent.

Understanding this pattern helps place modern developments in perspective. The shifts occurring in global finance today may feel dramatic, but Scripture reminds us that history has always moved through similar cycles.

Human systems rise and fall.

But the Kingdom of God remains.

Matthew 24:8 (KJV)

"All these are the beginning of sorrows."

Chapter 7
From Shaking to System
A Sequential View

In the previous chapters we explored how global instability can lead to the creation of new systems. We examined the growing pressures on financial structures, the rise of digital technologies, and the possibility of international coordination through bodies such as a Board of Peace. These developments raise an important question. How might such systems actually emerge in the real world?

Biblical prophecy often describes events that unfold through a process rather than a single dramatic moment. Jesus referred to coming troubles as "birth pains," suggesting a pattern where pressures increase gradually over time. Economic strain, technological expansion, political coordination, and spiritual conflict may develop step by step rather than all at once.

History also shows that major structural changes rarely appear suddenly. They tend to arise during seasons of instability, when nations and institutions search for solutions to problems that existing systems can no longer manage effectively.

The following progression is not presented as a prediction of exact events or timelines. Instead, it is a possible sequence that reflects patterns described in Scripture and trends visible in the modern world. Each stage builds upon the pressures created in the previous one, gradually shaping the conditions in which new global systems could emerge.

One possible progression may look like this.

Stage 1: Monetary Destabilization

The first stage in this progression begins with pressure inside the global monetary system. Modern economies are closely connected, and financial confidence plays a central role in keeping that system stable. When confidence begins to weaken, even slightly, the effects can spread quickly across markets and nations. Investors become cautious, governments reconsider financial strategies, and ordinary citizens begin to feel the strain through rising costs and economic uncertainty.

One area where this pressure can appear is in the stability of major global currencies. The United States dollar has long served as the primary reserve currency used in international trade. Because of this role, movements in the dollar influence financial conditions across the world. Periods of volatility can lead some nations to reconsider how heavily they rely on dollar based assets. In recent years, certain countries have gradually reduced their holdings of U.S. Treasury securities while exploring ways to diversify their financial reserves.

At the same time, central banks in various regions have increased their accumulation of gold. Gold has historically been viewed as a store of value during times of uncertainty. When nations increase their gold reserves, it can reflect a desire to protect national wealth against potential instability in currency markets or sovereign debt systems. This does not necessarily mean the existing system is collapsing, but it does indicate that some governments are preparing for the possibility of greater financial turbulence.

Inflationary pressure has also become a growing concern in many parts of the world. Rising prices affect nearly every aspect of daily life, including food, energy, housing, and transportation. When inflation remains elevated for extended periods, it reduces purchasing power and places stress on both households and national economies. Governments must then make difficult decisions as they attempt to balance economic growth with efforts to stabilize prices.

Together, these developments can create an environment where trust in long established financial systems begins to feel less certain. The global economy has experienced cycles of instability before, and such challenges do not automatically lead to systemic collapse. However, prolonged financial pressure often encourages policymakers and institutions to begin searching for alternative approaches that promise greater resilience and control.

Jesus described the early stages of global upheaval using the image of birth pains in Matthew 24. Birth pains begin gradually, but they grow stronger and more frequent as time progresses. In a similar way, economic instability may start with isolated disruptions before expanding into wider pressures that affect multiple regions at once. What begins as currency volatility or rising inflation can gradually interact with other challenges and intensify the strain on financial systems.

When financial uncertainty grows, governments and financial leaders naturally begin exploring new tools that might strengthen oversight, improve efficiency, and restore confidence in the system. In the modern world, those solutions increasingly involve digital financial technologies and new forms of economic infrastructure.

Stage 2: Digital Acceleration

As financial instability increases, governments and central banks begin looking for tools that promise greater stability, transparency, and control. In today's technological environment, many of those solutions are digital. When traditional systems show signs of strain, leaders often turn toward new financial technologies that can help them monitor activity more closely and manage risk more effectively.

One of the most widely discussed developments is the expansion of central bank digital currencies, often referred to as CBDCs. These are digital versions of national currencies issued and managed directly by central banks. Unlike traditional cash, which moves through physical exchange, digital currencies operate through electronic systems that can record and verify transactions almost instantly. Supporters often describe CBDCs as a way to modernize financial infrastructure, improve payment efficiency, and reduce the risks associated with fraud or illegal financial activity.

Alongside the development of digital currencies, many countries are gradually reducing their reliance on physical cash. In many parts of the world, people already use mobile payments, credit cards, and online banking for most daily transactions. As digital payments become more common, physical currency plays a smaller role in everyday commerce. Governments sometimes encourage this shift because digital transactions can be easier to track, regulate, and secure within the broader financial system.

Another important element in this transition involves digital identification systems. As more services move online, governments and financial institutions increasingly rely on secure digital identity frameworks to verify individuals. These systems may allow people to confirm their identity when accessing financial accounts, government programs, healthcare systems, or international travel. Digital identification can simplify many processes and help reduce fraud, but it also links personal identity more closely to financial and administrative networks.

Artificial intelligence is also becoming an important part of financial oversight. Modern financial systems generate enormous amounts of transaction data every day. Artificial intelligence tools can analyze that data far more quickly than traditional systems, identifying patterns that may signal fraud, cyber threats, or unusual financial behavior. Banks, regulators, and governments are increasingly using these technologies to monitor financial activity and respond to potential risks before they escalate.

Most of these developments are introduced gradually and often with little public attention. They are typically presented as improvements that make financial systems faster, safer, and more efficient. In many ways, these technologies do offer real benefits and can help address genuine challenges within modern economies.

Infrastructure, however, is rarely built overnight. Major systems are usually developed quietly over time, piece by piece, while societies focus on solving immediate economic problems. As digital currencies expand, cash becomes less central to everyday transactions, digital identity frameworks spread, and artificial intelligence takes on a greater monitoring role, a new financial architecture slowly begins to take shape.

Stage 3: Global Crisis Convergence

As digital infrastructure expands and financial systems become more connected, the global environment can also become more vulnerable to disruption. Interconnected systems bring efficiency and speed, but they also mean that crises in one area can quickly affect many others. When multiple pressures emerge at the same time, instability can spread far beyond a single nation or sector.

One form of disruption that has become a growing concern is cyber activity directed at financial institutions and critical infrastructure. Modern banking networks, payment systems, and financial exchanges rely heavily on digital platforms. While these systems allow transactions to move rapidly across borders, they can also become targets for cyber attacks designed to disrupt financial activity or create uncertainty in markets. Even the possibility of coordinated cyber incidents can raise fears about the resilience of the global financial system.

At the same time, regional conflicts continue to affect international stability. Wars or military tensions can disrupt trade routes, shift political alliances, and place pressure on global supply chains. When conflict occurs in strategically important regions, the consequences can reach far beyond the immediate battlefield. Energy supplies, shipping lanes, and international markets can all be affected.

Trade fragmentation is another factor that can intensify global instability. When nations impose tariffs, restrict exports, or separate into competing economic blocs, global trade becomes less predictable. Businesses may struggle to secure materials, manufacturing costs may rise, and international cooperation may weaken. Over time, these divisions can strain the economic relationships that have supported global growth for decades.

Energy disruptions can add another layer of pressure. Modern economies depend heavily on reliable energy supplies for transportation, manufacturing, and daily life. When energy production or distribution is interrupted, the effects can spread quickly through national economies. Rising energy prices can fuel inflation, slow economic growth, and create political tension within and between nations.

Each of these challenges on its own can strain the global system. When several occur at the same time, the impact can be far more severe. Financial instability, technological vulnerability, geopolitical conflict, and economic fragmentation can begin to interact with one another, creating an environment of widespread uncertainty.

In such moments, public concern often grows beyond national borders. Governments face pressure to respond quickly, while citizens look for reassurance that stability can be restored. As crises multiply and intersect, fear can spread across regions and economies, creating a sense that the challenges facing the world are no longer isolated but shared.

When fear becomes global, the demand for coordinated solutions often grows stronger. Nations that once acted independently may begin searching for ways to work together in order to restore stability and prevent further disruption.

Stage 4: The Board of Peace Emerges

When instability spreads across financial systems, technology networks, and geopolitical relationships, the pressure for coordination often grows stronger. Nations that once managed their affairs independently may begin to recognize that many modern challenges cross borders and require shared responses. In moments of widespread uncertainty, international cooperation is frequently presented as the most practical path toward restoring stability.

It is within this kind of environment that a multinational coalition could emerge with the stated goal of maintaining order and preventing further disruption. Such a body might be formed through agreements between major economies, international institutions, and regional alliances that seek to coordinate their efforts more closely. Its purpose would likely be described in terms of stability, security, and the preservation of global systems that support trade and economic activity.

One of the responsibilities of such a coalition could involve harmonizing currencies and financial standards. As digital currencies expand and traditional monetary systems face pressure, governments may seek ways to ensure that financial networks remain compatible and stable across borders. Coordinated policies could help prevent sudden disruptions in exchange systems and maintain confidence in global markets.

Another focus might involve protecting financial infrastructure from digital threats. As payment networks, banking systems, and economic platforms rely increasingly on technology, concerns about cyber sabotage grow more serious. A coordinated international framework could aim to strengthen defenses, share intelligence, and respond quickly to cyber attacks that threaten financial stability.

The coalition could also establish global compliance standards designed to regulate participation in financial and digital systems. These standards might address issues such as fraud prevention, financial transparency, and the responsible use of emerging technologies. By creating shared rules across multiple nations, such frameworks could attempt to ensure that financial systems remain secure and predictable.

Artificial intelligence governance may also become part of this effort. As AI technologies play a larger role in economic monitoring, financial decision making, and risk assessment, governments may seek ways to coordinate how these tools are used. Shared guidelines and oversight structures could be developed to manage AI systems that influence global markets and financial networks.

Throughout history, periods of crisis have often led to the consolidation of authority within larger governing structures. The book of Daniel describes a vision of kingdoms that eventually concentrate power in ways that affect the entire world. While interpretations of these passages vary, the imagery reflects a pattern where political authority becomes increasingly unified during times of upheaval.

In such a climate, the language used to describe new governance structures would likely emphasize peace, cooperation, and stability. Leaders would present coordination not as the loss of national independence, but as a necessary step toward protecting the global community from further crisis. In this way, peace becomes the banner under which new structures of authority are introduced.

Stage 5: Economic Authorization System

As international coordination expands and digital financial infrastructure becomes more widely established, the next development could involve systems that connect economic participation to verified identity. In a world where transactions are increasingly digital, the ability to buy, sell, or access financial services may become closely linked to identity verification within approved networks.

Digital identity systems are already being explored or implemented in many regions as a way to confirm who is participating in financial activity. These systems are often introduced to prevent fraud, strengthen security, and simplify access to services. When connected with digital currencies and global payment networks, identity verification can allow financial transactions to move quickly while ensuring that each participant is properly authenticated.

Artificial intelligence may also play a role in monitoring and evaluating activity within these systems. AI technologies are capable of reviewing large amounts of data in real time, identifying patterns, and flagging behavior that falls outside established guidelines. Financial institutions and regulators could use these tools to determine whether transactions meet compliance standards set within the broader system.

Over time, such technologies could create an environment where participation in economic activity depends on meeting certain conditions. Access to financial networks may be granted to those whose identities and activities align with established frameworks. At the same time, restrictions could be placed on accounts or transactions that fall outside those standards. In this way, participation in the economy could gradually become tied to authorization within a structured system.

Revelation 13 describes a future moment when buying and selling become connected to a form of approval within a governing authority. For many readers of Scripture, this passage has long served as a warning about the potential for economic control. As modern financial systems become more centralized and technologically integrated, some observers see parallels that raise questions about how such conditions might one day emerge.

Whether or not current developments represent the direct fulfillment of that prophecy remains a matter of interpretation. What is clear is that technology now makes it possible for financial participation to be monitored, authorized, or restricted in ways that were not possible in earlier generations.

Stage 6: Allegiance Becomes Visible

As systems of economic authorization expand and global governance structures grow stronger, the focus of the conflict may gradually shift. What once appeared to be primarily about financial stability, technology, or regulatory compliance could begin to reveal a deeper issue. At a certain point, the question may no longer center on currency systems or access to markets.

The deeper issue becomes allegiance.

Throughout history, systems of power have often required some form of loyalty from those who participate in them. When authority becomes centralized and participation is tied to compliance, individuals may eventually face choices that go beyond economic convenience. The question may shift from how one participates in the system to whom one ultimately gives their allegiance.

The New Testament speaks about a period of spiritual deception that precedes the revealing of a powerful opposing authority. In 2 Thessalonians 2, the apostle Paul describes a time when deception spreads widely before the truth becomes fully visible. This passage reminds believers that spiritual conflict often unfolds gradually, with confusion and persuasion appearing before the true nature of events becomes clear.

In such a setting, the central issue is no longer simply about economic participation or technological systems. Instead, it becomes a matter of worship and loyalty. Scripture repeatedly emphasizes that the ultimate conflict at the end of the age is not primarily political or financial. It is spiritual.

If the progression described in earlier stages were ever to unfold, the final challenge would likely reveal itself in this way. Participation in the system would no longer be merely administrative. It would involve recognition of authority and acceptance of its claims.

For believers, this stage highlights the importance of discernment and faithfulness. Systems may change, technologies may evolve, and political structures may rise or fall. Yet the call of Scripture remains constant. Followers of Christ are called to remain watchful, grounded in truth, and faithful in their allegiance regardless of the pressures surrounding them.

Revelation 14:12 (KJV)

"Here is the patience of the saints: here are they that keep the commandments of God, and the faith of Jesus. "

Chapter 8
When the System Demands Your Allegiance

For many people, the idea of global control or economic restriction sounds like something that would arrive suddenly and violently. Popular imagination often pictures dramatic events, open conflict, or sweeping government declarations that instantly change the world.

But systems rarely work that way.

Large systems tend to change gradually. Policies shift. Technologies evolve. Procedures expand. What begins as administrative updates or security measures can slowly reshape how people participate in everyday life. Most of the time, these changes appear ordinary at first. They arrive quietly, wrapped in the language of efficiency, safety, and modernization.

If a system of economic authorization were ever to emerge, it might not begin with force. It might begin with something far more familiar.

A notification.

A message appears on a screen.

Your account access has been restricted pending compliance review.

Your digital identification requires verification.

Your participation status is under evaluation.

At first, these kinds of messages might seem routine. Digital systems already send alerts for suspicious transactions, identity checks, or policy updates. Many people would simply follow the instructions, verify their information, and move on with their day.

Yet over time, systems designed to manage financial participation can also begin to determine who is allowed to take part and who is not. What began as a process of efficiency can slowly become a form of enforcement.

Throughout history, moments eventually arrive when systems require more than simple compliance. They require allegiance.

For believers, that moment is not entirely new. The early Christians who lived under the Roman Empire faced a similar tension. Rome governed vast territories and maintained order through political authority and cultural expectations. Most citizens were expected to acknowledge the emperor as a supreme authority within the empire.

Christians could live within that system. They could work, trade, and participate in society. But there was one line they could not cross.

They would not bow to Caesar as a divine authority.

Because of that decision, many believers paid a price. Some lost positions of influence. Others were excluded from economic and social opportunities. Still others faced imprisonment or death.

Yet while they lost security and status in the eyes of the empire, they held firmly to something far greater.

They did not lose eternity.

Efficiency Becomes Enforcement

Modern systems are designed to make life easier. Digital payments allow transactions to happen instantly. Identification systems help confirm who is accessing services. Artificial intelligence can monitor complex networks and detect problems long before human observers might notice them.

In many ways these innovations offer real benefits. They can reduce fraud, simplify transactions, and improve the speed at which information moves across financial systems. Governments and institutions often introduce these tools with the goal of strengthening stability and protecting the public.

Yet systems that increase efficiency can also expand oversight.

When financial activity moves through digital channels, transactions leave a record. When identities are verified through centralized platforms, access to services becomes easier to manage. Artificial intelligence systems can analyze vast amounts of data and identify behavior that falls outside established patterns.

These capabilities make it possible to detect threats and enforce rules with remarkable speed.

At first this may seem entirely reasonable. Financial networks have always required rules and safeguards. Banks monitor transactions for fraud. Governments establish regulations designed to protect markets and prevent crime. Digital tools simply allow these functions to operate more quickly and on a larger scale.

Over time, however, systems designed for convenience can also become systems of control.

When participation in financial networks requires verified identity, approved credentials, and continuous compliance, access to the economy itself can become conditional. A person's ability to buy, sell, transfer funds, or access services may depend on whether their status remains in good standing within the system.

Artificial intelligence can make these determinations almost instantly. Transactions can be approved, delayed, or denied within seconds. Accounts can be flagged, restricted, or suspended based on automated evaluations.

Efficiency then becomes enforcement.

What began as a tool for managing financial networks can gradually evolve into a mechanism that determines who is allowed to participate. And when participation depends on compliance with centralized systems, the line between administration and authority becomes increasingly important.

Eventually the question is no longer only about technology or regulation.

It becomes a question of allegiance.

The Moment of Personal Decision: The Line in the Sand

Systems can grow slowly. Policies expand, technologies evolve, and oversight increases step by step. For long periods, many people may not feel the impact of these changes in a personal way. Life continues, transactions move forward, and daily routines remain largely unchanged.

Yet history shows that there are moments when systems move from observation to demand. At some point participation may require more than simple compliance with administrative procedures. It may require agreement with the authority behind the system.

This is the moment when the line becomes visible.

For some people the decision may appear small at first. A request to acknowledge a requirement. A condition attached to participation. A choice between maintaining access to the system or standing apart from it.

For believers, such moments carry deeper meaning. The question is no longer simply about financial participation or technological compliance. It becomes a matter of loyalty and conviction.

Scripture often reminds believers that faithfulness is not proven when conditions are easy. It is revealed when pressure increases and choices become costly. When systems require actions that conflict with allegiance to Christ, followers of Jesus must decide where their loyalty truly rests.

Throughout history many believers have faced similar decisions. Some were asked to compromise their faith in order to maintain their place in society.

Others were pressured to adopt beliefs or practices that conflicted with their devotion to God.

In those moments the issue was never merely about social acceptance or economic opportunity. It was about allegiance.

The same principle applies in every generation. Systems may change. Technologies may advance. Political structures may rise and fall. Yet the fundamental question for believers remains the same.

Who ultimately holds our allegiance?

For the Christian, the answer has already been chosen. Allegiance belongs to Christ above every system, institution, or authority that may appear in the world.

When that moment arrives, the line in the sand becomes clear.

Lessons from the Early Church

The challenge of living faithfully within powerful systems is not new. The earliest Christians faced a similar reality under the Roman Empire. Rome governed vast territories and maintained authority through law, military strength, and cultural expectations. For most people, participation in Roman society meant recognizing the authority of the emperor and honoring the traditions that upheld the empire.

For Christians, this created a difficult tension. They were not rebels seeking to overthrow the empire. They worked, traded, raised families, and lived as citizens within Roman society. The teachings of Jesus and the apostles encouraged believers to respect governing authorities and live peaceably whenever possible.

Yet there was a line they could not cross.

Roman culture often required citizens to participate in acts that honored Caesar as a divine authority. Public ceremonies and civic rituals sometimes involved declarations of loyalty that went beyond political respect and entered the realm of worship.

For followers of Christ, this was a boundary they could not accept.

They could live within the empire, but they could not bow to Caesar as lord. Their allegiance belonged to Christ alone.

Because of this conviction, many believers faced difficult consequences. Some lost positions of influence or were excluded from social networks that required participation in imperial rituals. Others faced economic pressure when refusal to compromise their faith limited their opportunities to trade or conduct business.

In the most severe cases, believers were imprisoned or executed for refusing to renounce their faith.

Yet even in the face of these pressures, the early church remained steadfast. They understood that earthly systems, no matter how powerful they appeared, did not hold ultimate authority over their lives.

Some lost status.

Some lost security.

Some lost their lives.

But they did not lose eternity.

Their example continues to speak to believers today. The systems of the modern world may look different from those of ancient Rome, yet the underlying question remains the same. When loyalty to earthly authority conflicts with loyalty to Christ, believers must decide where their true allegiance lies.

The Systems of Our Time

The developments discussed throughout this book are not distant theories. Many of the trends shaping global systems are already visible in various forms across the world today. Financial systems are evolving, technology is expanding its reach, and nations are searching for ways to maintain stability in an increasingly uncertain environment.

One area of concern often discussed by economists is the long term stability of major global currencies. The United States dollar has played a central role in international trade for decades. Yet financial pressures, rising debt levels, and shifting economic alliances have led some analysts to question how global monetary systems may change in the future. If confidence in traditional structures weakens, the world may begin moving toward new economic frameworks.

At the same time, digital financial systems are advancing rapidly. Digital payment networks, central bank digital currency research, and electronic identification systems are reshaping how transactions occur. These technologies promise efficiency and security, but they also create new forms of oversight that can monitor financial participation more closely than ever before.

Artificial intelligence is also becoming deeply integrated into modern infrastructure. AI systems now analyze financial transactions, detect patterns of risk, and assist in regulatory compliance. These tools allow institutions to evaluate enormous amounts of data in real time, making financial systems faster and more responsive than previous generations could have imagined.

In addition to technological change, there are increasing discussions about international cooperation to manage global crises. Economic instability, cyber threats, regional conflicts, and energy disruptions have encouraged leaders to explore ways to coordinate responses across national borders. In such environments, multinational frameworks designed to promote stability may gain influence as nations seek solutions to shared challenges.

These developments can appear practical and even necessary in a complex global economy. Governments want to maintain financial stability. Institutions seek to protect infrastructure from disruption. Technologies are often adopted because they solve real problems.

Yet no system created by human authority carries ultimate power.

Economic structures may shift. Currencies may rise and fall. Technologies may transform the way societies operate. But none of these systems possess the authority to determine the final destiny of humanity.

No global system dethrones Christ.

The Sovereignty of Christ

Throughout history many systems have appeared powerful and permanent. Empires have risen with great authority, shaping the lives of millions and influencing the course of nations. Governments, economies, and technologies have all claimed the ability to bring stability and control to an uncertain world.

Yet every system built by human hands eventually changes.

Empires that once seemed unstoppable have faded into history. Economic systems that once dominated global trade have been replaced by new frameworks. Technologies that once appeared revolutionary have given way to newer innovations.

Scripture reminds believers that these shifts are not surprising. Human systems rise and fall within the flow of history, but they are never the final authority.

The book of Revelation describes a period when earthly power appears to concentrate in ways that challenge the faith of believers. The imagery of the Beast represents systems that demand loyalty and attempt to assert authority over human life and worship.

For many readers, these passages can feel unsettling. They describe a time when deception spreads widely and pressures increase for those who remain faithful to Christ.

But Revelation does not end with the Beast.

The story moves beyond the rise of earthly power to the ultimate victory of the Lamb. Christ is revealed as the true King whose authority surpasses every throne and system that exists in the world.

This truth has sustained believers throughout every generation. No government, economic structure, or technological system can replace the authority of Christ. His kingdom does not depend on human institutions, and it cannot be shaken by the changes that occur in the world.

When believers understand this, fear loses its power.

The events of history may be significant, and the developments discussed throughout this book may reshape the global landscape. Yet none of these changes alter the central truth that anchors the Christian faith.

Christ reigns above every system.

The Posture of the Christian Warrior

The final response for believers is not panic or fear. Scripture never calls followers of Christ to react to uncertainty with alarm. Instead, believers are called to remain watchful, grounded, and faithful regardless of the systems that rise around them.

The Christian warrior approaches the future with discernment. We recognize the times in which we live, but we do not lose our footing when systems shift. The world has always moved through seasons of change. Nations rise and fall, economic structures evolve, and technologies reshape how societies function.

None of these changes alter the foundation of the Christian faith.

The call for believers is to prepare their hearts, strengthen their faith, and remain anchored in truth. Preparation does not mean fear. It means spiritual readiness. It means understanding that faithfulness may require courage when systems begin demanding allegiance that belongs to Christ alone.

Throughout history believers have navigated powerful empires, economic systems, and political pressures. The circumstances have changed from generation to generation, but the posture of faith has remained the same.

Systems rise.

Currencies fall.

Technology evolves.

Yet the Kingdom of God remains unshaken.

Economic systems may transform the way people trade and interact. The decline of one currency may signal the birth of another financial order. Digital systems and artificial intelligence may reshape how societies organize their economies and institutions.

These developments may be historic.

But they are not ultimate.

The authority of Christ stands above every system built by human hands. No empire, government, technology, or financial structure has the power to dethrone the Lamb who reigns forever.

For the believer, this truth provides clarity and peace. The future may bring challenges, but it also carries the promise that the story of history does not end with human systems.

It ends with Christ.

I am Alpha and Omega, the beginning and the end, the first and the last."

— Revelation 22:13